THE OFFICIAL
MANCHESTER CITY ANNUAL 2017

g

A Grange Publication

©2016 Published by Grange Communications Ltd., Edinburgh, under licence from Manchester City Football Club. Printed in the EU.

Written by David Clayton Designed by Simon Thorley
Photographs ©ManCity (thanks to Victoria Haydn)

ISBN: 978-1-911287-09-4

Contents

MCFC 05

Welcome
PEP**GUARDIOLA**

Meet one of the best coaches in world football...

Pep Guardiola became City's new Head Coach this summer.
The 45-year-old Catalan, winner of 22 trophies in seven years as manager of Barcelona and Bayern Munich, succeeded Manuel Pellegrini who left the Club after three years in charge.
Pep, a father of three young children, signed a three-year contract after admitting City had been keen to bring him to the Etihad for several years.
He said: "I chose Manchester City because they have wanted me to come here for a long time. I know Txiki Begiristain and Ferran Soriano from my time at Barcelona and I am very happy to be here. I want to convince the players to be the best they possibly can be and I want not only our supporters to be very proud of the way we play football but football fans around the world."
So what do we know about our new boss?
Well, Pep comes with a record of success that few managers can match and since 2008, he has won 22 major trophies – that's an average of 2.75 trophies per season. Not bad! He has won the Champions League twice plus seven domestic titles with Barcelona B, Barcelona and Bayern Munich. Add two Copa Del Rey triumphs and two DFB-Pokal victories – the equivalent of the FA Cup in Spain and Germany plus three UEFA Super Cups and three FIFA Club World Cups. Quite a record!
Barca won the Spanish title three years in a row and the Champions League twice in Pep's time at the Nou Camp, when he worked with global superstars including Lionel Messi, Zlatan Ibrahimovic, Andres Iniesta and Yaya Toure. He also won the title three times in row with Bayern Munich where he had players such as Thomas Muller, Tony Kroos, Robert Lewandowski, Arjen Robben and Franck Ribery.
And Pep's success is not restricted to management - he won 18 different winner's medals during his playing career – all with Barcelona where he was a first team regular for more than a decade between 1990 and 2001. He also won 47 caps for Spain between 1992 and 2001, scoring five goals along the way. He made his debut against Northern Ireland in 1992 and his final match was against Mexico in 2001.
And with a Pep Guardiola side, you are guaranteed entertainment, great football and goals – plenty of goals if his record at Barca and Bayern is anything to go by! He has won 328 out of 450 matches as a coach with Barcelona B, Barcelona and Bayern Munich. Out of 450 matches, there have also been 77 draws and 45 defeats – a win percentage of 72.89% overall.
Barcelona and Bayern Munich scored 666 goals during Pep's time as manager – and an average of 2.62 goals per game. Pep has received 19 individual awards as a coach – these include La Liga Coach of the Year (x4) and FIFA World Coach of the Year.
Welcome to Manchester, Pep!

SEASON REVIEW 2015/16

Our month-by-month guide of City's season...

A look back to how last season panned out...
There were some highs and some lows in the 2015/16 season - but the truth is there were not enough highs and too many lows with injuries to key players making things even more difficult. So, going month by month, let's take a look at how things went...

AUGUST

City couldn't have started any better with four wins from four games – without conceding a goal! It was the form of champions and after comfortably beating West Brom and Chelsea 3-0, the Blues then recorded back-to-back 2-0 wins over Everton and Watford. With 12 points already on the board, City were flying.

SEPTEMBER

September began with a tricky away game at Crystal Palace and the game appeared to be heading for a 0-0 draw, until sub Kelechi Iheanacho scored a 90th- minute winner to preserve City's 100% record and make it five wins on the bounce – but that would be as good as it got for the Blues who would lose three of their next four games in all competitions. Losses to Juventus, West Ham and Tottenham took away the feel-good factor August had brought, though a 4-1 win at Sunderland and a 2-1 win away to Borussia Monchengladbach eased the disappointment.

OCTOBER

City needed to find their sparkle again – and quickly – so the start to October was exactly what the doctor had ordered. Newcastle were thrashed 6-1 at the Etihad with Sergio Aguero scoring an incredible five goals and after the international break, City again gave the Etihad fans a treat by beating Bournemouth 5-1. A 2-1 win over Sevilla was followed by a hard-fought – though dull – 0-0 draw away to Manchester United. The Blues finished the month with a 5-1 win over Crystal Palace in the Capital One Cup and a narrow 2-1 win over Norwich. Five wins, out of six and lots of goals – it seemed the Blues were back on track.

NOVEMBER

October's blistering form continued into November as City beat Sevilla 3-1 to all-but confirm progress to the Champions League Round of 16 with the best performance of the campaign so far – but it was followed by a dour 0-0 draw away to bottom of the table Aston Villa. Worse was to follow as the Blues were humbled at home to Liverpool with Jurgen Klopp's side deservedly winning 4-1. Then a 1-0 defeat to Juventus in Turin followed with only a 3-1 win and an improved display against Southampton repairing some of the damage inflicted by the previous three results.

DECEMBER

As Christmas approached, City had yet another mixed bag of results with consistency hard to come by – especially with Leicester City and Tottenham emerging as shock title rivals. Further progress in the cup competitions was secured with a 4-1 win over Hull City and a 4-2 victory over Borussia Monchengladbach, but a below-par 2-0 loss at Stoke further dented the Blues' title hopes. A 2-1 win over Swansea was followed by a 2-1 loss at Arsenal – and then a 4-1 win over Sunderland on Boxing Day had City fans scratching their heads wondering which Manchester City was going to turn up each week. The final result of 2015 was a 0-0 draw with Leicester City, who continued to set the pace at the top of the table.

JANUARY

It was vital City began the New Year strongly and a 2-1 win away to Watford was the perfect start. A 2-1 loss to Everton in the Capital One Cup semi-final first leg was not a disaster and a 3-0 FA Cup win at Norwich kept the quest for silverware ticking along nicely. But again, there was frustration after a 0-0 league draw with Everton at the Etihad saw the Blues lose further ground in the title race. Crystal Palace were beaten 4-0 in the next game before City took a decent point in a 2-2 draw away to West Ham United. And a 3-1 second leg Capital One Cup win over Everton secured a place in the final – though it came at a price as Kevin De Bruyne – one of the star performers of the season – was ruled out for 10 weeks with a knee injury. The Blues rounded off a fairly good month by beating Aston Villa 4-0 in the FA Cup thanks to an Iheanacho hat-trick.

FEBRUARY

In many ways, this was the make-or-break month for City and it started perfectly with a 1-0 win away to Sunderland, setting up the return clash with leaders Leicester City nicely, but all hopes of narrowing the gap at the top were dashed as the Foxes won easily at the Etihad running out 3-1 winners. Of all the defeats suffered so far, this was by far the most damaging and it got worse as Spurs further enhanced their own title hopes with a 2-1 win at the Etihad – back-to-back losses against the top two teams and hopes of winning the league were all-but over. Due to an important upcoming Champions League game, Pellegrini was forced to play a very young team in the FA Cup tie at Chelsea – effectively sacrificing hopes of progressing – and City lost a third match in a row after being beaten 5-1. At least a 3-1 win over Dynamo Kyiv meant City had one foot in the quarter-finals of the Champions League and a dramatic penalty shoot-out at Wembley secured the Capital One Cup to end the month on something of a high.

MARCH

Liverpool didn't have to wait long for revenge as they ended any lingering title hopes with a 3-0 win at Anfield, but a 4-0 home win over Aston Villa at least raised spirits. Relegation-threatened Norwich ground out a 0-0 draw at Carrow Road and City were uninspiring in the second leg against Dynamo Kyiv after another 0-0 draw – but at least it secured a place in the quarter-finals of the Champions League for the first time. But the Blues ended the month with a 1-0 home loss to Manchester United as suddenly finishing in the top four started to look unlikely.

APRIL

The return of Kevin De Bruyne from injury was just the boost City needed and with long-term absentee Samir Nasri also back, the Blues looked impressive in a 4-0 win at Bournemouth. Then an excellent first leg display away to Paris Saint-Germain with City earning a 2-2 draw was followed by a 2-1 win at home to West Brom. The Blues were suddenly looking back to their best and a 1-0 win over PSG in the return leg put City into the semi-finals of Europe's most prestigious club competition. Better still, a third successive Premier League win followed as City thrashed Chelsea 3-0 at Stamford Bridge with third spot in the table now the best Pellegrini's side could aim for. A 1-1 draw at Newcastle was followed by a 4-0 win over Stoke with Real Madrid the opposition in the UCL semi-final. A 0-0 draw at the Etihad was a reasonable result, but it gave the Blues a lot to do in the return.

MAY

Minds were perhaps elsewhere as the good form ended with a 4-2 defeat at Southampton, and a fortuitous Gareth Bale goal edged Real Madrid home in the Bernabeu with a nervy City left wondering what might have been. Hopes of finishing third in the Premier League were also ended as Arsenal claimed a 2-2 draw at the Etihad meaning City needed a draw from the final game to secure fourth spot ahead of United and a tense performance away to Swansea just edged the Blues home, with a 1-1 draw enough to secure a Champions League play-off round for 2016/17.

ILKAY **GUNDOGAN**

FACT FILE:
Nationality: German
Position: Attacking/Defensive Midfielder
Born: Gelsenkirchen, Germany, 24/10/1990
Previous clubs: Vfl Bochum II, FC Nurnberg, Borussia Dortmund II, Borussia Dortmund

German international Ilkay Gundogan joined City in June 2016 from Borussia Dortmund for whom he made 157 appearances over the past five seasons. The versatile midfielder has so far won 16 caps for Germany, scoring four goals, but missed Euro 2016 after injuring his knee before the tournament.

A box-to-box midfielder, Gundogan can operate anywhere in the middle of the park and will give incoming manager Pep Guardiola plenty of options.

Born in Gelsenkirchen, Ilkay started out with local side Schalke 04's youth team, moving on to SV Gelsenkirchen-Hessler 06 where he spent five years and then had a further year at SVV Buer.

Aged 15, he signed for Vfl Bochum, making his senior debut during the 2008/09 campaign. A couple more appearances for Bochum's second team followed before he moved to FC Nurnberg clocking up 53 starts between 2009 and 2011. Gundogan's talents then caught the eye of Borussia Dortmund boss Jürgen Klopp and the Bundesliga side paid around £3m for his services.

During his first year at Dortmund, he was an integral member of the side that won the Bundesliga and German Cup, playing 36 times and scoring four goals. His second campaign saw Dortmund reach the Champions League final, scoring his side's only goal from the penalty spot as Klopp's men lost 2-1 to Bayern Munich at Wembley. A back injury kept him side-lined for the majority of the 2013/14 season but he returned to have excellent campaigns – perhaps his best yet – in 2014/15 and 2015/16.

Need to Know: Ilkay Gundogan
Pass Master

Gundogan has earned a reputation for his sublime range of passing and will provide City with yet more attacking options, particularly from deep where he enjoys collecting the ball from the back four and threading eye-of-the needle passes through to the strikers. He is also strong, quick, can break up play and win back possession being particularly effective in a press. He is energetic and has an excellent work ethic, working just as hard without the ball as he does with it at his feet.

They said...

When Ilkay first signed for Dortmund, then-boss Jürgen Klopp said: "Ilkay brings a great attitude; he has a great passing game, is a complete player, and fits perfectly into our footballing system. He is willing to learn and is very smart."

He said...

"I'm thrilled to have signed for Manchester City. When I learned of City's interest my heart was set on coming here and things have moved very quickly. Now I have a new challenge and that is to achieve great things with City. The opportunity to work with a coach like Pep Guardiola is something I am really looking forward to and I am flattered to be the first signing the Club has made this summer. "I can promise the City fans I will give everything to help us win titles both in England and the Champions League. These are exciting times. I have my best years ahead of me and I think we can achieve great things together. I can't wait to begin this new chapter in my career."

New number?

Ilkay wore the No.8 jersey at Dortmund but unless he can convince Samir Nasri to swap, he will have to find a new squad number for City.

International pedigree

Gundogan has played at all levels for his country, winning caps at Under-18, Under-19, Under-20 and Under-21 level before making his debut for Joachim Low's senior squad in October 2011 in a 3-1 win over Belgium.

Summer Signing #2
NOLITO

FACT FILE:
Nationality: Spanish
Position: Forward/Winger
Born: Sanlucar de Barrameda, 15/10/1986
Previous clubs: Ecija Balompie, Barcelona B, Benfica, Granada (loan), Celta Vigo

Nolito became City's second signing of the summer after agreeing a four-year deal.

The Spain forward joined the Blues from Celta Vigo where he spent three seasons, scoring 39 goals in 103 appearances.

The 29 year-old also played for Pep Guardiola at Barcelona, though spent much of his time with the Catalans' B side from 2008 to 2011.

Able to play as a forward or winger, Nolito – real name Manuel Agudo Duran – began his career with Écija Balompié, playing 76 times between 2006 and 2008. From there he joined Barcelona B who had just been promoted to the second tier of La Liga under Pep Guardiola who left to coach the first team.

Nolito stayed with Barcelona B for three years, scoring 29 goals in 106 appearances before being promoted to the senior team under Guardiola, making five appearances in the 2010/11 campaign.

With first team opportunities restricted and despite being offered a five-year deal, Nolito opted to join Benfica, enjoying two campaigns with the Portuguese giants for whom he scored 16 goals in 63 starts.

Nolito was loaned to Granada for six months during the 2012/13 campaign before joining Celta Vigo on a permanent deal.

Consistently one of Celta Vigo's best players, he won his first international call-up at any level aged 28, playing in Spain's 1-0 defeat to Germany.

After making the preliminary squad for Euro 2016, he scored four goals in two games against Bosnia and South Korea and was named in the final 23-man squad as a result.

Nolito started all three of Spain's Euro 2016 group matches and is determined to make up for lost time with the national team, aiming to enjoy every minute of the experience.

Popular among team-mates and supporters alike, Nolito has battled hard to get to the top and is looking forward to a new chapter in his career.

Need to Know: Nolito

So what do we know about City's new Spanish recruit? Here's a few interesting facts you may or may not know about our new forward…

Keeping it real

Nolito comes from a working class background and says he is just a normal guy who tries to live a normal life. He said: "I try to be a normal person in spite of the repercussions of me being a footballer. I like messing about with friends; I know that when all this ends I will just go back to being somebody normal."

Much of this, no doubt, comes from his childhood where he was brought up by his grandparents Dolores and Manuel, living in a household of 12. His grandfather was a fishmonger and it was he who convinced Nolito to follow his dream of being a footballer – he lived long enough to see his grandson sign for his beloved Barcelona.

He dedicates every goal to Manuel as well as his partner Laura and daughter Lola.

Mini bash!
Nolito is not one for big cars and bling – he drove a mini to training at Celta Vigo and commented: "Of course, as footballers we get paid a lot, some more than others, but the greatest satisfaction comes from making people happy with the football you play. You can't buy that with all the money in the world."

Nolito had a job as a butcher's boy aged 13 and because his grandmother had 11 children, he has more than 30 cousins.

Downtime
When on international duty Nolito enjoys playing poker and listening to Flamenco music – apparently even more than Spain team-mate Sergio Ramos, often turning the music up loud for the enjoyment of his colleagues whenever it's played.

Debut boy
Nolito has earned a reputation for making memorable debuts for his new club. At Celta Vigo he took the corner that ended with Cristiano Ronaldo scoring an own goal and giving Celta their first win over Real for 40 years. At Benfica he scored successive goals in his first five matches, earning comparisons with the legendary Benfica star Eusebio, no less! He bagged two goals in his first game – a Champions League preliminary match with Trabzonspor.

Crossword

Can you solve the crossword below – all about last season? Trust us, it gets easier the more you answers you fill in!

ACROSS

03 Who dyed his hair blue then blonde last season?

06 This team knocked City out of the FA Cup

08 Who did Patrick Vieira leave City to coach?

09 Which club did Edin Dzeko leave City for?

10 Who is better known as 'El Mago'?

11 Which team beat City in the FA Youth Cup final for a second successive year?

12 Which club did Pep Guardiola last manage?

13 Which team did Sergio Aguero score five goals in one game against in 2015/2016?

15 Which team did Kevin De Bruyne sign from?

16 Which country does Ilkay Gundogan play for?

17 Which Tottenham player scored against City at home and away?

18 Joe Hart saved a penalty against this Swedish superstar last season - who was it?

19 Which country does Kelechi Iheanacho represent?

20 Which defender made his 300th appearance for City last season?

DOWN

01 Who was City's penalty-saving hero in the Capital One Cup final?

02 Which EDS player scored on his debut in the FA Cup tie away to Chelsea?

04 Who joined City from Liverpool last year?

05 City loaned Patrick Roberts to this Scottish club last season

07 Who did Nicolas Otamendi score his only goal against?

14 Whose goal knocked City out of the Champions League?

Answers on page 60&61

JESUS
NAVAS

GoalsoftheSeason2015/16

Here's ten unforgettable goals from last year's campaign with our ratings out of five for importance and technique...

FERNANDINHO
V CHELSEA
(August)

Importance:
****

Technique:
****

With City already 2-0 up, the Blues were looking for a third goal that would seal an impressive first home game of the new campaign and when David Silva intercepted a sloppy pass just outside the box he played the ball to Fernandinho who sent in a low angled drive from 18 yards that flew past the keeper and into the net.

SERGIO AGUERO
V CHELSEA
(April)

Importance:
***

Technique:
****

A goal made by Kevin De Bruyne and expertly finished by Sergio Aguero. De Bruyne picked up the ball on the edge of his own box before nonchalantly knocking it through two Chelsea players and powering forward. He released it at the perfect moment and Aguero did the rest with a smart finish inside the box.

KEVIN DE BRUYNE
V HULL CITY
(December)

Importance:
**

Technique:
*****

A free-kick Cristiano Ronaldo would be proud of. Kevin De Bruyne sent a howitzer of a shot over the Hull City wall and over a defender on the line. It had power, pace and dipped at the perfect moment.

YAYA TOURE
V WEST BROM
(August)

Importance:
****

Technique:
****

City made an impressive start to the campaign with a 3-0 win at West Brom and this goal was the pick of the bunch. Yaya Toure moved forward in the West Brom half before playing the ball to Wilfried Bony who passed it back into Yaya's path and the Ivorian sent a beautiful shot into the roof of the net from 18 yards.

KELECHI IHEANACHO
V SPURS
(February)

Importance:
****

Technique:
****

City were trailing 1-0 when substitute Kelechi Iheanacho equalised with a stunning finish from 10 yards. David Silva found Gael Clichy who sent in a clever low cross that Iheanacho thumped into the top corner of the net to briefly level the scores.

ALEKS KOLAROV
V BOURNEMOUTH
(April)
Importance: **
Technique: ****

There seemed little danger when Aleksandar Kolarov picked the ball up on the left wing. But the Serbian cut inside before ghosting past two defenders and rifling an unstoppable left-foot thunderbolt into the top right-hand corner of the net to complete a 4-0 win over the Cherries.

RAHEEM STERLING
V BOURNEMOUTH
(October)
Importance: ***
Technique: ****

Kevin De Bruyne picked the ball up in his own half, moved forward and spotted the run of Raheem Sterling who latched on to the pass, cut inside one defender who recovered to challenge again – only to be beaten again – and Sterling dummied a shot that fooled another defender and the goalkeeper, before firing home a low shot.

SERGIO AGUERO
V WATFORD
(January)
Importance: ****
Technique: ****

With City trailing 1-0 eight minutes from time, Yaya Toure equalised and suddenly an unlikely win was on. Two minutes later, Navas found Bacary Sagna whose deep cross hung in the air for Sergio Aguero to send a spectacular header past Gomes for a dramatic winner for City.

YAYA TOURE
V DYNAMO KYIV
(November)
Importance: *****
Technique: ****

City had been cruising at 2-0, but Kyiv pulled one back and were battling to get back on level terms in the first leg of the Champions League Round of 16 tie in the Ukraine. With just a couple of minutes left, Yaya Toure picked the ball up, played a one-two with Fernandinho before curling a wicked drive into the top corner to seal the victory.

KEVIN DE BRUYNE
V NEWCASTLE
(October)
Importance: ***
Technique: *****

A cracking goal by the Belgian maestro – it began when Jesus Navas spotted De Bruyne's run and chipped a fine pass into the box where De Bruyne acrobatically sent a cushioned volley over the goalkeeper and into the far top corner of the net.

Wordsearch#1

See how many City players you can find in our Wordsearch – remember, the words could be horizontal, vertical or diagonal!

```
O G W O W N N P T K V W W B A L
H Y I H L A R C M W M X V N W D
C N D N M G C R T D Q M G K M J
A A N I L O D K F R B A L V N K
N P E D G D B C J T S K D Q E O
A M M N N N Y G Q Y L P M V R N
E O A A M U C P R W G D I E M P
H K T N Y G W A V T Z N U B K P
I T O R W Y C P D N D G W X P K
I N S E N A P Y F E A Q V T T G
H E A F B K N V B O W Q X K L W
C C L D M L Q R I Y Y K P R M Q
E N O G M I U G K G V K V H G M
L I C V R Y R W J B N N P G K R
E V I W N E D A V I D S I L V A
K G N E S B J K M D V D H F P W
```

Bacary Sagna
David Silva
Fernandinho
Ilkay Gundogan
Kelechi Iheanacho

Kevin De Bruyne
Nicolas Otamendi
Sergio Aguero
Vincent Kompany

KEVIN DE BRUYNE

What a stunning first season for the talented Belgian...

City were reportedly interested in Kevin De Bruyne for quite some time, with the Blues continually linked with the Belgian play-maker but as August drew to a close, a deal for the 2014/15 Bundesliga Footballer of the Year and German Footballer of the Year 2015 still hadn't been finalised – then, much to the relief of the City fans, De Bruyne's capture was officially confirmed as a Manchester City player, taking the No.17 shirt.

An international break meant he had to wait until mid-September to make his debut - away to Crystal Palace - replacing the injured David Silva from the bench and soon settled into life in the Premier League, scoring on his full home debut against West Ham United.

De Bruyne scored further goals against Sunderland and Tottenham to secure the Etihad Player of the Month award for September. It would be the first of four such Club awards during his first campaign in sky blue.

KDB's ability to pick a pass along with his vision, crossing ability and habit of scoring crucial goals quickly made him a huge favourite among the City fans. Going into the New Year, many believed De Bruyne was a contender for the PFA Player of the Year award, but in the second leg of the Capital One Cup semi-final against Everton, he landed awkwardly and injured his knee and ankle and was ruled out for two months – during that time, City won just five of the next 12 games and as a result, the Blues' title chances all-but ended.

De Bruyne's return from injury saw City enjoy their best month of the season, winning five and drawing two of the seven games played and it was KDB's crucial goals in the Champions League that saw City through to a historic first semi-final in the competition. De Bruyne scored City's opening goal in Paris and then the only goal in the 1-0 win over PSG at the Etihad.

Though City didn't progress past Real Madrid, De Bruyne ended his first campaign with 16 goals and 14 assists from the 41 games he played – an amazing return, but not a surprise given that he scored 16 goals and made 28 goals during his final season with Wolfsburg! No wonder he is coveted throughout Europe and such a favourite in his own country.

So impressed was City's Club Ambassador Mike Summerbee, a Manchester City legend from the late 1960s and early 1970s, that he claimed De Bruyne was the closest thing to Colin Bell – regarded as the Club's greatest player – that he'd ever seen. High praise indeed!

Under Pep Guardiola, De Bruyne is expected to kick on again and is expected to become a pivotal part of what everyone hopes will be a new exciting era for the Blues.

De Bruyne was voted the Etihad Player of the Season, beating Sergio Aguero (second) and Fernandinho (third).

ONE TO WATCH:
BRAHIM DIAZ
BORN: MALAGA, SPAIN (03/08/1999)
POSITION: ATTACKING MIDFIELDER

Brahim Diaz is regarded as one of the most exciting prospects emerging from the Club's Academy.

The gifted midfielder joined the Blues from Malaga as a 14 year-old with City fighting off interest from Barcelona for this most precocious of talents.

A clever midfielder who enjoys collecting the ball deep and carrying it forward, Diaz is capable of breath-taking dribbles and superb technique.

His idol is Lionel Messi who he admits he studies closely, Diaz also cites David Silva as one of his major influences, often seeking his advice.

Diaz played for the City Under-19s last season featuring in the UEFA Youth League home games against Sevilla and Borussia Monchengladbach – scoring in the latter.

His star continued to shine at the UEFA European Under-17s Championships in Azerbaijan last summer where he was one of the stars of the tournament.

Diaz helped Spain reach the final, scoring three goals along the way including one in the final itself where he also successfully converted a penalty kick in the resulting shoot-out with Portugal – though Spain ultimately lost 5-4.

The teenager has admitted he is excited by the prospect of working with Pep Guardiola – the Barca coach that gave Messi his debut aged 17 and he could become a regular fixture for the Elite Development Squad in 2016/17.

And who knows? If Guardiola sees enough potential, we may see Diaz in and around the first team sooner rather than later…

ONE TO WATCH:
BERSANT CELINA
BORN: PRIZREN, FR YUGOSLAVIA (09/09/1996)
POSITION: ATTACKING MIDFIELDER

Bersant Celina is expected to challenge for a regular place in the first team squad in 2016/17 with the talented play-maker already appearing three times for the senior team.

Intelligent with great vision, Celina is also a free-kick specialist and has scored several stunning goals at EDS level.

Celina grew up in Norway after his family moved to the country when he was aged two. Aged 15, he played for Norwegian side Stromsgodset where he was soon spotted by City who offered him a scholarship to come to England.

He signed his first pro contract in July 2014 and though he was named as a sub for the first team in January 2015 for the visit of Sheffield Wednesday – almost exactly a year later he made his debut after coming on as sub in the FA Cup tie away to Norwich. He then made his Premier League debut a month later in a home defeat to Leicester City – assisting a Sergio Aguero goal.

A fortnight later he made his full debut away to Chelsea and signed a new four-year deal in May 2016. Though he'd represented Norway at Under-15, 16, 17 and 21 level, when Kosovo were permitted to play friendly matches against other FIFA members, Celina accepted the call-up to play for Kosovo and has so far made three appearances. Celina has not ruled out representing Norway at senior level in the future.

Will Celina get more opportunities in 2016/17 or will he gain experience by going out on loan? Watch this space…

DAVID
SILVA

MCFC 28

Spot the Ball#1

Can you spot the ball? We've removed the real ball from the picture below so you'll have to use detective work to try and figure out exactly which grid it's in – it's tricky and maybe not as obvious as it first looks.

Answers on page 60&61

Summer Signing #3
GABRIEL JESUS

Teenage sensation Gabriel Jesus won't be a Manchester City player until 2017, though the Blues and Palmeiras agreed the transfer in the summer.

Jesus completed the campaign with his Brazilian side before moving to Manchester where he is expected to join the squad for the second half of the season.

Aged 19, Jesus is tipped as the 'next big thing' in his homeland, with the Palmeiras forward has been compared to superstar Neymar by some football writers, though it is obviously too early to say how high his star might rise.

It was reported that Manchester United and Barcelona also made offers for Jesus, but the opportunity to work with Pep Guardiola was too good to refuse for the Brazil international who took part in the Rio Olympics last summer.

An exciting talent, he is versatile across the forward line and has the ability to score thrilling individual goals with his vast array of technical ability. Definitely one for the future, City may have acquired one of the most coveted South American talents of recent years.

Summer Signing #4
MARLOS
MORENO

Colombian striker Marlos Moreno became a City player during the summer with the teenager signing from Atletico Nacional on a five-year deal.

Joining new arrivals Gabriel Jesus and Leroy Sane, the 19 year-old is yet another players signed with an eye on the future.

Moreno won't arrive at the Club until the 2017/18 season at the earliest as he was immediately loaned out to La Liga side Deportivo La Coruna for the 2016/17 season.

Moreno progressed through the youth system at Atletico and had earned seven full caps for Colombia going into the 2016/17 season and like many of the Blues' new signings, he said Pep Guardiola was a big reason he decided to sign.

"Guardiola is one of the best managers in the world. I think he likes young players very much and he can improve young players tactically and technically. It will be great to work with him and to be part of a great team."

Another versatile, hard-working forward, City fans will be keeping a close eye on his progress in Spain this year.

Manchester City Capital One Cup Winners 2016

City won the Capital One Cup for the second time in three years. In a thrilling finale, the match went to penalties after drawing 1-1 with Liverpool. The Blues won 3-1 thanks to three fantastic saves by Willy Caballero to win the trophy.

2017 THE BIG CITY QUIZ

40 questions to test your City knowledge… award yourself a point for each correct answer - but some carry extra bonus points for difficulty – there's a total of 60 points available!

I. True or false?
Kevin De Bruyne could have represented Burundi instead of Belgium? *(1 POINT)*

2. Which manager decided not to sign Pep Guardiola as a player?
A) Stuart Pearce
B) Kevin Keegan *(1 POINT)*

3. How many goals did Sergio Aguero score in all competitions last season? *(2 POINTS)*

4. Which club did Jason Denayer spend the 2015/16 season on loan with? *(2 POINTS)*

5. True or false?
Yaya Toure has never missed a penalty for City *(1 POINT)*

6. Which country did David Silva win his 100th cap against?
Czech Republic or Georgia? *(1 POINT)*

7. Which team did Kelechi Iheanacho score his first senior hat-trick against?
(2 POINTS)

8. True or False? Jesus Navas joined City from Osasuna
(1 POINT)

9. Who knocked City out of the FA Cup?
(2 POINTS)

10. How many City players were at Euro 2016?
A) 5 B) 7 C) 9
(2 POINTS)

11. What was the final score in the Capital One Cup penalty shoot-out?
(2 POINTS)

12. Samir Nasri scored two goals last season – can you name the clubs he scored against?
(3 POINTS)

13. Which club did City sign Patrick Roberts from?
(2 POINTS)

14. Which Real Madrid player scored a goal against Joe Hart at Euro 2016?
(1 POINT)

15. Who did Sergio Aguero score five goals against in one game last season?
(1 POINT)

16. Who scored two goals on his 21st birthday last season?
(2 POINTS)

17. Who has scored City's first goal of the season for the past three years?
(3 POINTS)

18. Martin Demichelis scored one goal in his final season with the Blues – but who was it against?
(1 POINT)

19. True or false? Manchester City Women finished third in the FAWPL last season
(1 POINT)

20. Who did England play in a friendly at the Etihad?
(2 POINTS)

21. Which of these clubs has Fabian Delph NOT played for?
A) Leeds United B) Stoke City
C) Aston Villa
(1 POINT)

Answers on page 60&61

22. Which EDS central defender made his debut away to Chelsea last season? *(2 POINTS)*

23. True or false? City scored the most Premier League goals in 2015/16 *(1 POINT)*

24. Who did EDS midfielder Manu Garcia score his first senior goal against? *(2 POINTS)*

25. Name the two players who ended the season as City's joint-top scorers in the Champions League. *(2 POINTS)*

26. How many successive clean sheets did City start the 2015/16 campaign with? A) 4 B) 5 C) 6 *(1 POINT)*

27. How many opposition players scored own goals against City last season? A) 1 B) 3 C) 5 *(2 POINTS)*

28. Which City player was credited with an own goal in the second leg of the Champions League semi-final against Real Madrid? *(1 POINT)*

29. Which City player celebrated passing 10million followers on Twitter in June 2016? *(1 POINT)*

30. How many City players were shown red cards in 2015/16? A) 0 B) 1 C) 2 *(1 POINT)*

31. Which team did Jesus Navas score his only goal of 2015/16 against? *(1 POINT)*

32. Raheem Sterling scored a hat-trick against which club? *(1 POINT)*

33. Which team did Joe Hart join City from?
(1 POINT)

34. What sea creature is also the nickname of Fernando?
(2 POINTS)

35. True or false? Tottenham boss Mauricio Pochettino and Pablo Zabaleta were once team-mates at Espanyol
(1 POINT)

36. Can you name the three players who successfully converted a penalty in the 2015/16 Capital One Cup shoot-out?
(3 POINTS)

37. Sergio Aguero's nickname 'Kun' comes from:
A) A family name
B) A cartoon character
C) A famous footballer
(1 POINT)

38. What was the official colour name of City's luminous change strip last season?
A) Ghost green
B) Spook yellow
C) Luminous spectre
(1 POINT)

39. Which country was Raheem Sterling born in?
(1 POINT)

40. Which club did Nicolas Otamendi join City from?
(1 POINT)

SCORE CHECKER:

60-50 – If Pep Guardiola needs advice, he can come to you!

49-30 – Solid campaign – deal extended by 1 year

29-20 – The board expected better... but no action taken

19-10 – The board are inviting applications

10-0 – Sorry, you're sacked with immediate effect!

Answers on page 60&61

Summer Signing#5
JOHN STONES

FACT FILE:
Nationality: English
Position: Central defender
Born: Barnsley 28/05/1994
Previous clubs: Barnsley, Everton

City's determination to recruit the most exciting young talent in world football continued with the signing of John Stones who joined City from Everton on 9 August 2016.

Regarded as one of the world's most promising centre backs, Stones spent more than three years at Everton where he built a reputation a classy defender who had maturity beyond his 22 years.

His passing from the back in particular caught the eye and his seemingly unflappable nature singled the Yorkshireman out as something special.

He began his career with hometown club Barnsley, making 28 appearances in total for the Tykes.

Everton were first to spot his potential and the Toffees snapped up the teenager on a five-and-a-half-year deal on the final day of the 2013 January transfer window.

Stones didn't make his senior debut for the Toffees until the following season when, on 28 August 2013, he appeared in the League Cup win over Stevenage and his Premier League bow followed a month later as a late substitute in their 1-0 victory against Chelsea.

That was one of 26 games he took part in during the 2013/14 season and he made two more than that in 2014/15, scoring his first Premier League goal against Manchester United in April 2015 towards the end of a season in which he earned a nomination for Europe's "Golden Boy" award – a title that eventually went to Raheem Sterling.

Stones made his full England debut on 30 May 2014 in a 3-0 friendly victory over Peru at Wembley.

Need to Know: John Stones

Stones is more than capable of filling in at right-back if required and began his career as something of a swashbuckling right-back for Barnsley. He played in that position a number of times for Everton and said: "I'll never rule out playing right-back because the more positions you can play the better it is for you and your team. I love to play centre back but I'll never rule out playing right-back because it's a great string to have."

Barcelona defender Gerard Pique picked Stones in his 'World XI' last November. Pique said: "Being a centre-back is not just about defending or being nasty or tough. It's about knowing how to play football, control the ball, pass and be more comfortable in possession. This is something they didn't understand in England 10 years ago, but now there is Stones. He is one of the new generation who understand football not just as a defender."

Stones has a reputation for being calm under the most difficult situations, often passing his way out of trouble rather than hoofing the ball clear – the very qualities that brought him to the attention of Pep Guardiola. He even took a 'Panenka' penalty against Juventus aged 19 – a gentle dink over the keeper that quickly gained him attention for being a little more than your average centre-half! Apparently, he can also do a mean impersonation of his team-mates and coaches, so watch out…

They said...

"He's incredible on the ball – I haven't seen another English player who's got the ability to start play in that manner – he can be left one v one, he's very good in the air, he reads the game fantastically well and he's got a terrific ability to adapt to different partners." Roberto Martinez

He said...
I'm absolutely delighted to sign for City and now the deal is done I'm looking forward to the next stage in my career. I've obviously seen what's going on here at the Etihad, it's an ambitious Club with a great manager so I can't wait to get stuck in and help achieve the goals we are aiming for."

New number?
John has opted for the No.24 shirt for his first season with City.

International pedigree:
Though he travelled with the England squad to Euro 2016, Roy Hodgson didn't use the young centre-half. Stones, who had won 10 full England caps prior to the 2016/17 season, is expected to become a mainstay in new England manager Sam Allardyce's side in the coming years.

Summer Signing #6
LEROY SANE

FACT FILE:
Name: Leroy Sane
Nationality: German
Position: Attacking midfielder/winger
Born: Essen, Germany 11/01/1996
Previous clubs: Schalke

Tipped as one of the hottest prospects in Europe, Leroy Sane joined City in August 2016. Having attracted interest from the continent's footballing giants, the attacking midfielder made the switch from Germany to England in a bid to continue his football education.

A bright young talent, his versatility proved a major attraction. He is able to play on either wing, as well as a number 10 or even a 'false 9'. He is tricky on the wing with excellent dribbling skills and loves nothing more than to put the ball through a defenders legs!

Sane rose to fame after breaking through Schalke's highly respected academy to their first team in 2014. His senior debut arrived in April against VfB Stuttgart – his only appearance that year – but since then, he has blossomed, becoming a first team regular and quickly built up a reputation as a Bundesliga talent to watch

He caught the eye in a visit to Manchester back in the 2014/15 season, playing for Schalke's under-19s against Patrick Vieira's City EDS in the UEFA Youth League. The German side's best moves came through the forward and he certainly stood out as one for the future.

At senior level, he wrote his name into the history books in March 2015 with a stunning strike to edge Real Madrid in a memorable 4-3 win in the Champions League, during a season in which he made 42 appearances and scored nine goals. With dual French and German citizenship, he had the option to represent either country, eventually opting for his birth nation Germany, making his first-team debut against France in November 2015 and was called up to the Euro 2016 side which reached the semi-final stage.

He follows in the footsteps of Ilkay Gundogan in making the move from Germany to Manchester and is the latest in a long tradition of German players who have graced the sky blue shirt.

Need to Know: Leroy Sane
City fans will take quickly to Sane – a direct and quick winger, he attempted 100 dribbles in the 2015/16 Bundesliga season – more than anyone other player, As well as scoring spectacular goals, he makes plenty for his team-mates, too. Only Dele Alli (19), Ousmane Dembele (17) and Anthony Martial (16) were directly involved in more goals than Sane (14) of all players aged 21 or under in Europe's top five leagues last season. He is versatile, too. Pep Guardiola likes his players to be capable of playing in a number of positions and Sane can fill a number of forward roles and isn't afraid to track back and help the defenders. An explosive talent – watch him go!

They said...
'Leroy Sane is a class player. I want him to shine with my assists, My aim is the title. To reach this it's important we have new players like Sane or Gundogan.' Kevin De Bruyne

He said...
"I think Pep Guardiola can make me a more complete player. I think I will need a bit of time to start with because it's another league and there's a different style of play but I think I can adapt very quickly."

New number?
Leroy has taken the vacant No.19 shirt for the 2016/17 season – the same number he had while at Schalke.

International pedigree:
Sane was a member of the Germany squad at Euro 2016 and had won four full caps going into the new season. He earned 11 Under-19 caps for his country and a further four at Under-21 level and is expected to be a major part of Coach Joachim Low's squad for the 2018 World Cup qualifiers.

TRAINING GROUND FUNNIES

Jokes and antics from the City training sessions

1: Martin and Pablo react to the claim that England will win the next World Cup. Harsh!

3: "Should you tell Vincent that I put superglue on his glove or should I?"

2: The Gaffer's always first in line for lunch!

4: "Don't look now Samir but the gaffer's come in wearing his slippers!"

Wordsearch#2

Here's another Wordsearch to solve – this time it's about the nationalities of some of our players during the 2015/16 campaign. Find the 10 words and remember, the words could be horizontal, vertical or diagonal...

```
L   N   A   I   B   R   E   S   T   C   B

C   N   F   N   B   B   J   Y   A   T   E

G   Q   B   R   R   Q   C   N   N   S   L

E   N   G   L   A   N   D   G   I   A   G

J   T   L   G   H   N   E   G   T   O   I

T   H   R   D   N   R   C   B   N   C   U

L   G   V   I   M   X   R   E   E   Y   M

G   Z   A   A   Y   A   V   R   G   R   Y

Q   P   N   R   Z   T   G   N   R   O   C

S   Y   X   I   H   G   R   Z   A   V   R

T   X   L   T   A   I   R   E   G   I   N
```

Argentina   Nigeria   Ivory Coast
Spain   France   Serbia
England   Belgium
Germany   Brazil

Answers on page 60&61

KEVIN
DE BRUYNE

SERGIO
AGUERO

NAME: CLAUDIO BRAVO
POSITION: GOALKEEPER
SQUAD NUMBER: 1

DATE OF BIRTH: 13/04/1983
PREVIOUS CLUBS: REAL SOCIEDAD, BARCELONA

2015/16 APPS (ALL COMPS):
0
2015/16 GOALS (ALL COMPS):
0
TOTAL CITY CAREER:
PLAYED: 0 GOALS: 0

BRAVO

NAME: WILLY CABALLERO
POSITION: GOALKEEPER
SQUAD NUMBER: 13

DATE OF BIRTH: 28/09/1981
PREVIOUS CLUBS: BOCA JUNIORS, ELCHE, ARSENAL SARANDI (LOAN), MALAGA

2015/16 APPS (ALL COMPS):
13
2015/16 GOALS (ALL COMPS):
0
TOTAL CITY CAREER:
PLAYED: 20 GOALS: 0

CABALLERO

NAME: JOHN STONES
POSITION: DEFENDER
SQUAD NUMBER: 24

DATE OF BIRTH: 24/05/1994
PREVIOUS CLUBS: BARNSLEY, EVERTON

2015/16 APPS (ALL COMPS): 0
2015/16 GOALS (ALL COMPS): 0
TOTAL CITY CAREER: PLAYED: 3 GOALS: 0

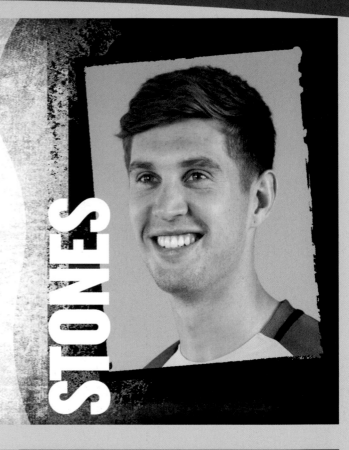

STONES

NAME: VINCENT KOMPANY (CAPTAIN)
POSITION: CENTRE-BACK
SQUAD NUMBER: 4

DATE OF BIRTH: 10/04/1986
PREVIOUS CLUBS: ANDERLECHT, SV HAMBURG

2015/16 APPS (ALL COMPS): 22
2015/16 GOALS (ALL COMPS): 2
TOTAL CITY CAREER: PLAYED: 288 GOALS: 14

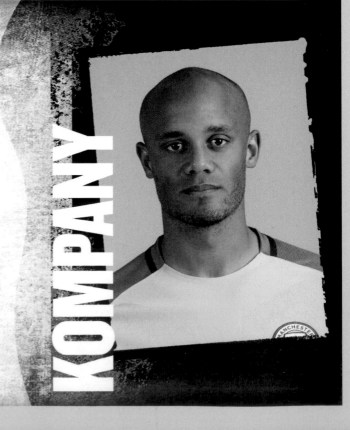

KOMPANY

NAME: NICOLAS OTAMENDI
POSITION: CENTRAL DEFENDER
SQUAD NUMBER: 30

DATE OF BIRTH: 12/02/1988
PREVIOUS CLUBS: VELEZ SARSFIELD, PORTO, VALENCIA, ATLETICO MINEIRO

2015/16 APPS (ALL COMPS):
46
2015/16 GOALS:
1

TOTAL CITY CAREER:
PLAYED: 48 GOALS: 1

OTAMENDI

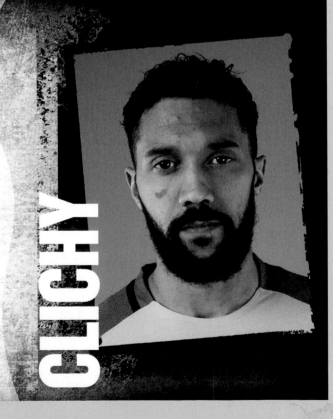

NAME: GAEL CLICHY
POSITION: LEFT-BACK
SQUAD NUMBER: 22

DATE OF BIRTH: 26/07/1985
PREVIOUS CLUBS: CANNES, ARSENAL

2015/16 APPS (ALL COMPS):
26
2015/16 GOALS (ALL COMPS):
0

TOTAL CITY CAREER:
PLAYED: 164 GOALS: 1

CLICHY

NAME: PABLO ZABALETA
POSITION: RIGHT-BACK
SQUAD NUMBER: 5

DATE OF BIRTH: 16/01/1985
PREVIOUS CLUBS: SAN LORENZO, ESPANYOL

2015/16 APPS (ALL COMPS):
21
2015/16 GOALS (ALL COMPS):
0
TOTAL CITY CAREER:
PLAYED: 282 GOALS: 9

ZABALETA

NAME: BACARY SAGNA
POSITION: RIGHT-BACK
SQUAD NUMBER: 3

DATE OF BIRTH: 14/02/1983
PREVIOUS CLUBS: AUXERRE, ARSENAL

2015/16 APPS (ALL COMPS):
45
2015/16 GOALS (ALL COMPS):
0
TOTAL CITY CAREER:
PLAYED: 61 GOALS: 0

SAGNA

NAME: ALEKSANDAR KOLAROV
POSITION: LEFT-BACK
SQUAD NUMBER: 11

DATE OF BIRTH: 10/11/1985
PREVIOUS CLUBS: CUKARICKI, OFK BEOGRAD, LAZIO

2015/16 APPS (ALL COMPS): 32
2015/16 GOALS (ALL COMPS): 3
TOTAL CITY CAREER: PLAYED: 200 GOALS: 20

KOLAROV

NAME: ILKAY GUNDOGAN
POSITION: MIDFIELD
SQUAD NUMBER: 8

DATE OF BIRTH: 24/10/1990
PREVIOUS CLUBS: NURNBERG, BORUSSIA DORTMUND

2015/16 APPS (ALL COMPS): 0
2015/16 GOALS (ALL COMPS): 0
TOTAL CITY CAREER: PLAYED: 0 GOALS: 0

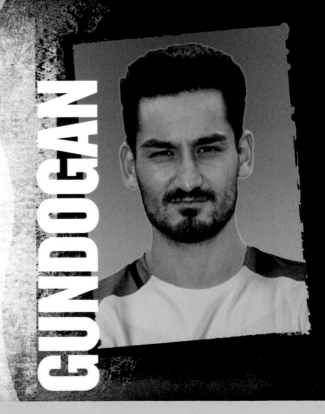

GUNDOGAN

NAME: LEROY SANE
POSITION: MIDFIELD
SQUAD NUMBER: 9

DATE OF BIRTH 11/01/1996
PREVIOUS CLUBS: BAYER LEVERKUSEN, SCHALKE

2015/16 APPS (ALL COMPS): 0
2015/16 GOALS (ALL COMPS): 0
TOTAL CITY CAREER:
PLAYED: 0 GOALS: 0

SANE

NAME: FERNANDO
POSITION: CENTRAL MIDFIELD
SQUAD NUMBER: 6

DATE OF BIRTH: 25/07/1987
PREVIOUS CLUBS: VILA NOVA, ESTRELA AMADORA (LOAN), PORTO

2015/16 APPS (ALL COMPS): 36
2015/16 GOALS (ALL COMPS): 2
TOTAL CITY CAREER:
PLAYED: 69 GOALS: 4

FERNANDO

NAME: FERNANDINHO
POSITION: CENTRAL MIDFIELD
SQUAD NUMBER: 25

DATE OF BIRTH: 04/05/1985
PREVIOUS CLUBS: ATLETICO PARANAENSE, SHAKHTAR DONETSK

2015/16 APPS (ALL COMPS):
46
2015/16 GOALS (ALL COMPS):
5
TOTAL CITY CAREER:
PLAYED: 139 GOALS: 72

FERNANDINHO

NAME: JESUS NAVAS
POSITION: ATTACKING MIDFIELD
SQUAD NUMBER: 15

DATE OF BIRTH: 21/11/1985
PREVIOUS CLUBS: SEVILLA

2015/16 APPS (ALL COMPS):
50
2015/16 GOALS (ALL COMPS):
1
TOTAL CITY CAREER:
PLAYED: 147 GOALS: 8

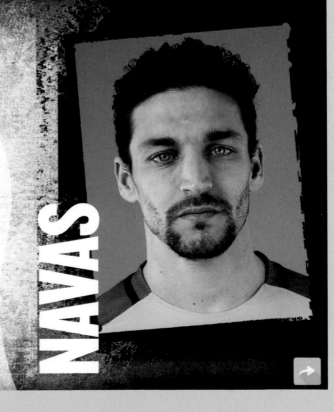

NAVAS

NAME: FABIAN DELPH
POSITION: MIDFIELD
SQUAD NUMBER: 18

DATE OF BIRTH: 21/11/1989
PREVIOUS CLUBS: LEEDS UNITED, ASTON VILLA

2015/16 APPS (ALL COMPS):
27
2015/16 GOALS (ALL COMPS):
2
TOTAL CITY CAREER:
PLAYED: 27 GOALS: 2

DELPH

NAME: YAYA TOURÉ
POSITION: CENTRAL MIDFIELD
SQUAD NUMBER: 42

DATE OF BIRTH: 13/05/1983
PREVIOUS CLUBS: SK BEVEREN, METALURH DONETSK, OLYMPIACOS, MONACO, BARCELONA

2015/16 APPS (ALL COMPS):
47
2015/16 GOALS (ALL COMPS):
8
TOTAL CITY CAREER:
PLAYED: 270 GOALS: 57

TOURE

NAME: KEVIN DE BRUYNE
POSITION: ATTACKING MIDFIELD
SQUAD NUMBER: 17

DATE OF BIRTH: 28/06/1991
PREVIOUS CLUBS: GENK, CHELSEA, WERDER BREMEN (LOAN), WOLFSBURG

2015/16 GOALS (ALL COMPS): 41
2015/16 GOALS (ALL COMPS): 16
TOTAL CITY CAREER: PLAYED: 41 GOALS: 16

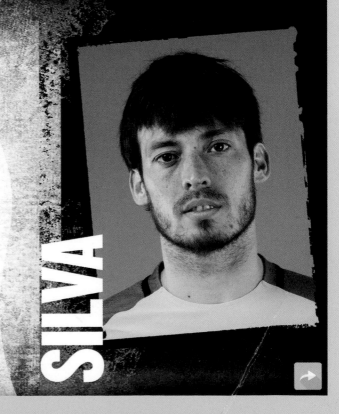

DE BRUYNE

NAME: DAVID SILVA
POSITION: ATTACKING MIDFIELD
SQUAD NUMBER: 21

DATE OF BIRTH: 08/01/1986
PREVIOUS CLUBS: VALENCIA, EIBAR (LOAN), CELTA VIGO (LOAN)

2015/16 APPS (ALL COMPS): 39 + 3 SUB
2015/16 GOALS (ALL COMPS): 12
TOTAL CITY CAREER: PLAYED: 263 GOALS: 39

SILVA

NAME: RAHEEM STERLING
POSITION: MIDFIELD
SQUAD NUMBER: 7

DATE OF BIRTH: 08/12/1994
PREVIOUS CLUBS: LIVERPOOL

2015/16 APPS (ALL COMPS):
46
2015/16 GOALS (ALL COMPS):
6
TOTAL CITY CAREER:
PLAYED: 46 GOALS: 6

STERLING

NAME: SERGIO AGUERO
POSITION: STRIKER
SQUAD NUMBER: 10

DATE OF BIRTH: 02/06/1988
PREVIOUS CLUBS:
INDEPENDIENTE, ATLETICO MADRID

2015/16 APPS (ALL COMPS):
44
2015/16 GOALS (ALL COMPS):
29
TOTAL CITY CAREER:
PLAYED: 208 GOALS: 136

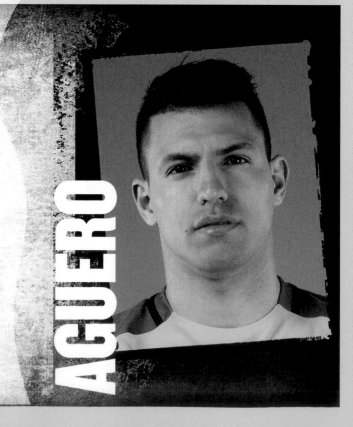

AGUERO

NAME: NOLITO
POSITION: FORWARD
SQUAD NUMBER: 9

DATE OF BIRTH: 15/10/1986
PREVIOUS CLUBS: SANLUQUENO, VALENCIA

2015/16 APPS (ALL COMPS):
0
2015/16 GOALS (ALL COMPS):
0
TOTAL CITY CAREER:
PLAYED: 3 GOALS: 2

NOLITO

NAME: KELECHI IHEANACHO
POSITION: STRIKER
SQUAD NUMBER: 72

DATE OF BIRTH: 03/10/1996
PREVIOUS CLUBS: NONE

2015/16 APPS (ALL COMPS):
35
2015/16 GOALS (ALL COMPS):
14
TOTAL CITY CAREER:
PLAYED: 35 GOALS: 14

IHEANACHO

Guess Who?

Here are four mystery City players – use your powers of observation and detective work to discover who they are

Quiz&PuzzleAnswers

CROSSWORD#1
(From page 18)

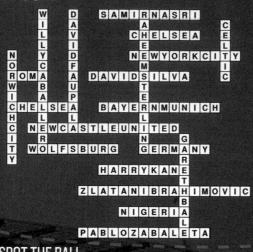

SPOT THE BALL
(From page 29)

ANSWER = A2

WORDSEARCH#1
(From page 23)

THE BIG CITY QUIZ 2017 - ANSWERS
(From page 34-37)

1. TRUE
2. A) STUART PEARCE
3. 29
4. GALATASARAY
5. TRUE
6. CZECH REPUBLIC
7. ASTON VILLA
8. FALSE- SEVILLA
9. CHELSEA
10. B) 7
11. 3-1 TO CITY
12. EVERTON AND WEST BROM
13. FULHAM
14. GARETH BALE
15. NEWCASTLE UNITED
16. RAHEEM STERLING
17. DAVID SILVA
18. BORUSSIA MONCHENGLADBACH
19. FALSE - THEY FINISHED SECOND
20. TURKEY
21. B) STOKE CITY
22. TOSIN ADARABIOYO
23. TRUE
24. CRYSTAL PALACE
25. KEVIN DE BRUYNE AND RAHEEM STERLING
26. B) 5
27. B) 3

28. FERNANDO

29. SERGIO AGUERO

30. A) 0

31. EVERTON

32. BOURNEMOUTH

33. SHREWSBURY TOWN

34. OCTOPUS

35. TRUE

36. JESUS NAVAS, SERGIO AGUERO, YAYA TOURE

37. B) A CARTOON CHARACTER

38. A) GHOST GREEN

39. JAMAICA

40. VALENCIA

WORDSEARCH#2
(From page 44)

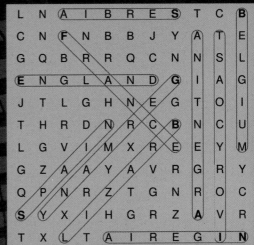

GUESS WHO?
(From page 58)

1 Fernando

2 De Bruyne

3 Aguero

4 Otamendi

WHERES MOONCHESTER?
(From page 62)

Winner!

Last year's winner Hannah Jimenez with her signed shirt and Official Manchester City Annual